Customer Service Excellence:

It's in the Details

Lisa Ford

American Media Publishing
4900 University Avenue
West Des Moines, Iowa 50266-6769
800/262-2557

Customer Service Excellence:
It's in the Details

Lisa Ford

Copyright © 1997 by American Media Inc. and Lisa Ford.

This publication is designed to provide accurate and authoritative information in regard to the subject matter covered. It is sold with the understanding that neither the author nor the publisher is engaged in rendering legal, accounting, or other professional service. If legal advice or other expert assistance is required, the services of a competent professional should be sought.

Credits:
American Media Publishing: Art Bauer
                               Todd McDonald

Managing Editor: Karen Massetti Miller
Designer: Gayle O'Brien
Cover Design: Polly Beaver

Published by American Media Inc.
4900 University Avenue
West Des Moines, IA 50266-6769

Library of Congress Catalog Card Number 97-77105
Ford, Lisa
Customer Service Excellence: It's in the Details

Printed in the United States of America
1997
ISBN 1-884926-83-5

Introduction

Many companies claim that customer service is their first priority, yet few follow through on this promise. Providing exceptional customer service gives your company a competitive edge. Exceptional customer service does not come from a marketing brochure or from the company president's speech. Exceptional customer service is given by each and every employee, each and every day. You are the reason your company stands apart from the competition.

"Quality in a service or product is not what you put into it. It is what the client or customer gets out of it." *Peter Drucker*

Customer service means different things to different customers. For the busy executive, it may mean prompt delivery at a reasonable price. For the office manager, it may mean a reliable service plan. For the lonely retiree, it may mean conversation and helpfulness. All of us would agree we want polite, courteous service. But is that enough?

Think of the people you have encountered who have delighted you with their exceptional customer service. One of my favorite customer service stories involves my business associates, Carla and Joe, who had driven several hours to attend a business meeting in another state. They knew they would be late arrivals, so they called three times to confirm that a hotel room would be held for them. But when they arrived at the hotel, all the rooms were gone. However, the clerk did have a suite on the concierge level available.

When Carla and Joe got to the suite, they entered the living area and opened up the door to the next room. To their surprise, they discovered another couple in the bedroom! Carla called the front desk, and hotel staff explained that they were sending a roll-away bed to the living area—this would be Carla and Joe's "room." By this time, they were tired and furious.

Joe headed back to the front desk to straighten the situation out. On his way, he met a janitor in the elevator. The janitor could tell Joe was frustrated and took the matter into his own hands. He apologized for the service Carla and Joe had received so far and acquired the key for another suite from the front desk. He then helped Carla and Joe move their suitcases to the new suite (complete with bed). That janitor was a service superstar, not to mention Carla and Joe's hero that late evening. Service stars have something in common—they care!

In business today, a satisfied customer is your best strategy. Getting a customer is easy. Keeping a customer is difficult. Let's find out how you can make the difference in your organization.

About the Author

Lisa Ford is a speaker and seminar leader with 18 years of experience presenting to businesses, associations, and government. She speaks throughout the United States and internationally on the topics of customer service; customer retention; and managing, hiring, and training for service excellence. Lisa is the creator of the best-selling business video series *How to Give Exceptional Customer Service.* She recently created the video *Customer Service Excellence: It's in the Details* for Business Advantage Inc.

Lisa's customer service experience began when she started working part-time jobs at age 14. After graduating from the University of Tennessee, she worked for a consulting firm, and in 1983, she started her own business as an independent speaker and seminar leader. Lisa is also actively involved with the National Speakers Association and serves as a Board Member to the College of Arts and Sciences at the University of Tennessee.

● Table of Contents

Chapter *One*

Why Customer Service?

Chapter Objectives

▶ Describe the difference between *traditional* and *exceptional* customer service.

▶ Identify what a customer wants.

▶ Discuss how customers' expectations influence their perceptions of service.

▶ Predict how positive and negative points of contact influence the customer's perception.

Today, with more and more competitors vying for your customers' attention, exceptional service is no longer optional—it's essential. When we think of customer service, we traditionally think of businesses in the service sector, such as restaurants, retailers, or health care providers. Today, most businesses have established customer service initiatives. Customer service is a key issue for:

Business

◆ Retail

◆ Business to business

◆ Professional

◆ Service and support

Government

◆ Local, state, and federal agencies

Not-for-profit agencies

- Community service

- Health centers

- Volunteer organizations

Some people are surprised when they hear that government and not-for-profit agencies are concerned about customer service, yet it is both possible and appropriate for these organizations. The American Cancer Society competes with other charities for both fundraising dollars and volunteers. They have an extensive training program for volunteer leaders and staff on how to creatively recruit and keep volunteers. And how do you think they keep volunteers? By treating them like valued customers.

Who Are Your Customers?

One of the first things any organization must do is identify their customers. This is not always as easy as it seems, since most organizations have two main sets of customers:

- Internal customers

- External customers

Both types of customers require exceptional customer service.

The *internal customer* is the individual or department within your organization who uses your products or services. By enhancing your customer service skills, you develop better working relationships with the people within your organization, as in the following example:

> ■ Steve is responsible for ordering forms and envelopes for the mailing services department of his company. Although ultimately his company's customers are those people who receive a mailing, Steve's primary customers are internal— members of the marketing department, word processors, computer programmers, and employees in his own mailing department. All his internal customers rely on Steve to purchase the products they need in a timely fashion. If Steve does not order the correct products, none of the internal departments can serve their external customers.

The *internal customer* is the individual or department within your organization who uses your products or services.

The *external customer* is the person or organization who purchases and uses your products and services.

The *external customer* is the person or organization who purchases and uses your products and services. This is the customer we traditionally think of; the external customer is the main focus of this book. In government and not-for-profit organizations, these are the people who use your services, along with the taxpayers and donors who support you. In business-to-business relationships, external customers may also be people with whom you are in a joint venture.

There is also another type of customer—one that many people find surprising. I am talking about your *former customer*—that person who, for one reason or another, does not do business with your organization anymore.

Former customers are an important resource. They have a great deal of information your organization can use to provide exceptional service. They can tell you:

◆ What your organization did wrong.

◆ What your organization did right.

◆ What, and how, your organization can improve.

Former customers have a great deal of information your organization can use to provide exceptional service.

Former customers have one other important characteristic— they are also potential future customers. Remember that, and reach out to them. Discuss with your coworkers how you might do so.

How Customer Service Has Changed

The nature of customer service has changed during the last 10 years. In the past, we provided what I will call *traditional customer service*. If customers needed service, they went to the Customer Service Department. The unspoken message to the customer was, "This department is the only place you'll get customer service in this company."

Customers hoped that a customer service employee would be able to meet their needs as competently and quickly as possible; however, this was not always the case. Very often, customers encountered a clerk who recited company policies about why he or she couldn't solve the problem. The clerk's main objective seemed to be helping the customer understand the Customer Service Department's limitations, not service.

1

Today's customers expect something more than traditional customer service. They demand *exceptional customer service.* They want us to exceed their expectations, demonstrate that the organization cares for the them, and work immediately and decisively on their behalf.

At first glance, there may not seem to be that much of a difference between traditional and exceptional customer service. But as you read this book, you will understand that there are critical differences. You will also begin to see how you, the service professional, make the difference between merely satisfying the customer and dazzling the customer with exceptional customer service.

Your competitors may easily be able to copy your products, your prices—even your promotions. But they can't copy *you* and the *service* you provide. You are the key. To your customer, you're the voice and the personality of your organization. As the person who deals with customers on a day-to-day basis, you come to signify all that your company stands for, both good and bad.

The ultimate goal of exceptional customer service is to maintain and increase market share through increased customer satisfaction. This means helping more customers, selling more products, or providing more services.

As a service provider, you are an important part of this equation. When customers are receiving service, they don't know the end result. They don't know whether you're going to say yes or no, or whether you're going to meet their time frame. But they do know and observe how the service is being delivered. It is the service delivery that matters!

> **The ultimate goal of exceptional customer service is to maintain and increase market share through increased customer satisfaction.**

There is only one boss—the customer. And he can fire everybody in the company, from the chairman on down, simply by spending his money somewhere else.
Sam Walton, founder of Wal-Mart

Take a Moment

There are several roles you play when assisting the customer. When you explain how a product or service works, you are a teacher. When you are trying to figure out what a customer needs, you are a detective. Think about the roles you play, and write down three roles you perform when working with customers.

1. _____

2. _____

3. _____

What Do Your Customers Want?

Let's look at what the customers want—how they define exceptional customer service. First, customers want you to listen. This shows concern and respect. Customers also want you to take responsibility. They do not want to hear what you cannot do or whose fault it is. They want you to walk them through the problem and to find a solution.

Customers expect you to pay attention to the details. Take notes if possible while listening to the customer. Then, paraphrasing the information, repeat back to the customer the key points. Make sure you have the details right, and give the customer an opportunity to correct or clarify any of the information.

Customers want to know that they're appreciated. Do not forget the sincere "Thank you" and "We appreciate your business." Although you may have said it to 100 other customers that day, your current customer still needs to hear it.

Customers want you to remember that they are spending their time and their money with you, and that both are valuable.

Finally, customers want you to remember that they are spending their time and their money with you, and that both are valuable. You're not doing *them* a favor; they are doing *you* one. Everything you do must be seen from the customer's perspective. After all, it is how the customer perceives you that determines what level of service you are actually providing.

Exceptional customer service is in the eyes of the customer. How does the customer determine whether you have provided exceptional customer service? It all depends on two things: the customer's expectations and the customer's perception.

Customer Expectations

Customer expectations are what a customer wants before a transaction. A customer forms expectations from several different sources:

> *Customer expectations are what a customer wants before a transaction.*

◆ **Advertising**—Advertisements can set specific expectations for your company. For many years, Domino's Pizza advertised that they would deliver your pizza within 30 minutes or the pizza was free. Your expectation was that you would have a pizza at your door in fewer than 30 minutes.

◆ **Previous experience**—Your customers' previous experiences with your product, services, or organization can influence their expectations about future service. If their last experience was negative, they'll expect the same in the future and may therefore decide to take their business elsewhere. If their last experience was positive, they'll look forward to more positive experiences when they bring you return business.

◆ **Word of mouth**—What your customers say about the quality of your service can build or ruin your organization's reputation, as in the following example.

   ■ Cindy planned meetings at several different hotels. Most hotels gave excellent or at least adequate service. But the catering director at one hotel always gave Cindy a difficult time. He reluctantly granted her requests and rarely returned her calls. Cindy became so frustrated that she began to dread every encounter at this hotel. Eventually, she pulled all her company's business. Unfortunately for this hotel, Cindy also discouraged other meeting planners from scheduling events there.

◆ **The competition**—Your competition can also set expectations for your customer. If a competitor offers a product at a certain price, or offers a free service, your customers come to expect the same from you.

Customer Perceptions

Customer perceptions are created during and after a transaction. A customer's perception is based on how your service measured up against her or his expectations. If customers get more than they expected, the end result is exceptional customer service.

However, if customers get anything less than they expected, they perceive a performance gap, and in that gap lies customer disappointment.

Exceptional Customer Service = Perception - Expectations

Disappointed customers will leave your organization and take their business elsewhere, and poor customer service is responsible for much of the disappointment experienced by customers:

◆ The Forum Corporation reports that 70 percent of the identifiable reasons why customers stop doing business with an organization has nothing to do with product. Customers surveyed reported that they left because they received a lack of personal attention, were treated rudely, or found an employee unhelpful.

◆ Another study done by the White House Office of Consumer Affairs and Technical Assistance Research Program (TARP) suggests that 68 percent of customers who quit doing business with an organization do so because of perceived indifference on the part of employees.

Once a customer becomes dissatisfied with your organization, it can be difficult to win him or her back. Research suggests that it takes 12 positive incidents to make up for one negative incident in the eyes of a customer. Replacing dissatisfied customers with new customers is also difficult. It costs five times as much to attract a new customer as it does to keep a current customer.

Take a Moment

Think about a positive customer service experience. What impressed you the most? How can you give the same type of experience to your customer? Now think about a negative service experience. Have you ever delivered this type of service? What can you do to avoid providing negative service again?

_____

_____

_____

Creating Positive Points of Contact

In doing business with your organization, customers have many points of contact, and they have a chance to form an impression of your organization at each point. These impressions can be good (*positive* or *winning points of contact*) or bad (*negative* or *breaking points of contact*). Examples of negative points of contact include letting your phone ring five or six times before answering it or leaving the customer on hold for a long period of time. This says, "We don't value your time." Long lines, out-of-stock items, faded signs, and dirty surroundings give customers the impression that your organization doesn't care about them. The customer may also wonder whether you care about the product or service.

> **Customers form an impression of your organization at each each point of contact.**

A caring and friendly atmosphere, ownership of problems, and quick solutions all create positive points of contact. Clean, neat surroundings, whether in an office, store, or restaurant, say, "We pay attention to details." Accurate invoices, shipping by dates promised, and returning phone calls promptly also convey a positive impression.

Make sure that all your points of contact with customers are positive ones. Give all your customers special attention, regardless of the size of their purchases. After all, the customer who makes a small purchase today might make a large purchase tomorrow. All your customers deserve exceptional service.

Take a Moment

Rate your customer service. Suggested responses appear on page 91.

1. What type(s) of customers do you deal with?
   a. Internal customers
   b. External customers
   c. Both

2. How do your customers feel after dealing with you?
   a. Better about your organization
   b. Worse
   c. The same

3. If a customer has a problem or concern, how quickly do you return his or her phone call?
   a. By the end of the business day
   b. Within 24 hours
   c. Within 48 hours
   d. Within 72 hours
   e. Within a week
   f. No set time

4. The old slogan says that the customer is always right. In reality, what do you feel customers are?
   a. Always right
   b. Sometimes right
   c. Generally wrong
   d. Misguided or misinformed

5. When you are delivering your organization's product or service, what is the most important thing?
   a. Price
   b. Customer service
   c. Product or service effectiveness
   d. Repeat business
   e. Customer perception
   f. Marketing strategies

1

Chapter Summary

Customer service has become a key issue for business, government, and not-for-profit agencies. Your *internal customers* are the individuals or departments within your organization who use your products or services. Your *external customers* are the persons or organizations who purchase and use your products and services.

When we provide *traditional customer service,* we meet customer expectations as competently and quickly as possible. When we provide *exceptional customer service,* we exceed customer expectations, demonstrate that the organization cares for the customer, and work immediately and decisively on the customer's behalf. The ultimate goal of exceptional customer service is to maintain and increase market share through increased customer satisfaction.

Customers determine that you have provided exceptional customer service based on their *expectations* and their *perceptions.* Customer expectations are what a customer wants before a transaction. Customer perceptions are based on how your service measures up against customer expectations.

Customers have the chance to form impressions of your organization whenever they have a point of contact with an employee. When those points of contact are negative, customers form bad impressions; when those points of contact are positive, customers form good impressions. A caring and friendly atmosphere, ownership of problems, and quick solutions are all positive points of contact that work to create a good impression.

Self-Check: Chapter 1 Review

Answers to the following questions appear on pages 91 and 92.

1. Define *internal customers.*

   _____

   _____

2. Define *external customers.*

   _____

   _____

3. How do we provide exceptional customer service?

   _____

   _____

4. What are *customer expectations?*

   _____

   _____

5. What are *customer perceptions?*

   _____

   _____

6. Fill in the following equation:

   Exceptional Customer Service = _____ - _____

7. Describe an example of a positive point of contact a customer can have with an organization.

   _____

   _____

Chapter *Two*

Creating a Positive Total Service Experience

Chapter Objectives

▶ Define the *total service experience.*

▶ Treat customers as partners by putting their needs first.

▶ Create a positive attitude by engaging in positive self-talk.

▶ Build strong customer relationships through effective communication.

As we saw in Chapter 1, every interaction you have with a customer is a point of contact. Customers can perceive those points of contact as positive or negative. As customers have more and more contacts with your organization, they combine their perceptions of those contacts into an overall impression of your organization's customer service. This impression is the customer's *total service experience.*

The best way to ensure that customers remain loyal to your organization is to be sure that they have a positive total service experience—and that can be a challenge. After all, the customer is the one who decides whether a point of contact with your company has been positive or negative. Creating the total service experience is like a game in which the customer makes all the rules and keeps score. Whether you and your organization win, or even get to keep playing, is completely up to the customer.

As a customer service representative, your job is to provide service that will help your customers have a positive total service experience. Although there is no guarantee that a customer will perceive a specific point of contact as positive, there are three basic techniques that customer service professionals practice to create the best impression possible:

◆ Treat your customer as a partner.

◆ Maintain a positive attitude.

◆ Communicate effectively with your customer.

2

Treating Your Customer as a Partner

■ Bob knew he needed to talk with his customer service representative about his order: It was a day late, and he needed the merchandise immediately. But he dreaded making the call. It would just be the same old runaround. He could almost hear his rep now: "I sorry, but I can't do anything about that. Here's why . . ."

Customers sometimes perceive customer service representatives as standing between them and the solution to their problems. This type of attitude is based on the traditional customer service model we discussed earlier in which the customer service representative focused on explaining the organization's limitations.

Providing exceptional customer service means working with your customer to create a solution for his or her problem. There are several ways you can treat your customer as a partner in the problem-solving process. The first is to ask yourself two key questions:

◆ What results does my customer want?

◆ How can I help my customer get these results?

Keep these questions in mind as you talk to your customer. Focus on what needs to be done to meet your customer's needs instead of explaining what the organization cannot do.

A second technique that will help you treat your customer as a partner is to respond to problems quickly. On-the-spot resolution is best. When you handle a problem on the spot, customer satisfaction increases. If you need to get assistance from a supervisor, explain to the customer that you need to get additional information and will return with an answer. Give the customer a specific time you will call back with the information,

Providing exceptional customer service means working with your customer to create a solution for his or her problem.

Respond to your customers within 24 to 48 hours.

and make sure you meet the deadline. The ironclad law of customer feedback says to respond within 24 to 48 hours. Even if you don't have a complete answer, let the customer know that progress is being made, and more importantly, that attention is being paid.

Is the responsive approach effective? Research clearly shows that if the customers believe you are responsive to a problem, they will do business with your organization again 82 to 95 percent of the time. In fact, loyalty to you will actually increase because you were so responsive. When you value their business and show you care, customers return.

A third technique for partnering with your customers is to beg for complaints. That's right—encourage your customers to bring their complaints to you. If you find out what your customers think, you can make your service even better. After you have heard a customer's concerns or suggestions on how your organization can improve its service or product, analyze the information. If you are unable to do anything about the suggestion yourself, pass the information along to the appropriate people—they will appreciate the input. If the suggestion involves something you can change, put together an action plan to make the appropriate improvements. This can be a formal written plan or just a reminder written on your calendar to follow through with a customer request.

Take a Moment

List the top five reasons you think customers buy from you instead of the competition:

1. _____

2. _____

3. _____

4. _____

5. _____

Once you have completed this list, ask two or three customers why they buy from you. Compare their responses to the responses above.

Developing a Positive Attitude

People who give exceptional customer service have a positive, can-do attitude. A positive attitude is not necessarily something you're born with. That's good news because it means that even if your attitude is currently negative, you can create an attitude that is helpful and dedicated to being exceptional.

It may sound simplistic, but the first step toward creating a positive attitude is to begin thinking positive thoughts about ourselves and others. The second step is to reflect those thoughts in *positive self-talk.*

Self-talk is something that happens inside, whether you are aware of it or not. We all talk to ourselves, and this self-talk can have a tremendous effect on your attitude. Positive self-talk can help you build a positive, winning attitude, while negative self-talk can do just the opposite.

Unfortunately, much of our self-talk is negative. We become our own worst enemies by telling ourselves things like:

- "I'll never be any good at this."

- "I look terrible today."

- "I'm sure that person hates me."

We need to change our self-talk to reflect positive thoughts and emotions. Think how much better you'd feel if you replaced the statements above with these:

- "I'm sure I can do this with just a little practice."

- "I look and feel great today."

- "I'm sure that person will like me once he gets to know me."

As your positive attitude develops, you'll find yourself wanting to improve your customer service performance. Customer service stars continually look for ways they can improve by asking themselves:

- "How am I doing?"

- "How can I improve?"

- "What should I be doing differently?"

Their answers to these questions help them provide their customers with a positive total service experience.

> Positive self-talk can help you build a positive, winning attitude, while negative self-talk can do just the opposite.

2

23

Take a Moment

For the next week, begin every morning by answering the following questions:

How am I doing?

_____

_____

How can I improve?

_____

_____

If there were one thing I could do differently, what would it be?

_____

_____

Providing exceptional customer service has a hidden beauty all its own that will help you maintain a positive attitude. You'll feel it at the end of the day when the last customer has been served and you're on the way out the door. You'll be energized, more positive in your overall attitude, and happier. You see, exceptional customer service is not only good for business, but a far more enjoyable and satisfying way to work.

When we seek to discover the best in others, we somehow bring out the best in ourselves.

William Arthur Ward

Communicating Effectively with Your Customers

In every point of contact with the customer, you communicate something—but unfortunately, it may not be the right thing. Consider the following example:

■ Consuela had just purchased a new printer for her computer. She tried to hook up the printer to her system, but she discovered that the cable that came with the printer was not the type she needed. She returned to the computer store and spoke with a clerk at the customer service counter.

"Yes, we can help you," the customer service representative said in a monotone. "Just leave the old cable here with me and go back and pick out a new one," she added without looking up from her paperwork.

Consuela felt uncomfortable as she walked back to pick out a new cable. She was relieved that the store would give her the cable she needed, but the way the customer service representative spoke to her made her wonder if they really valued her business.

When we think about communicating, we usually think of the words we say. But as the previous example illustrates, your body language, tone of voice, and words must match in order for your communication to be effective.

Body Language

Does your body language support what your words say? You may tell a customer that you are happy to help him or her, but if you frown, slump, or refuse to make eye contact, the customer will not believe you. This is because people are more likely to believe nonverbal signals, such as a frown, than words.

> **People are more likely to believe nonverbal signals, such as a frown, than words.**

Use these simple tips to convey your concern for customers through your body language:

◆ Smile and nod your head to encourage the customer to speak.

◆ Lean slightly forward and maintain eye contact with the customer to show that you are interested in what she or he has to say.

♦ Avoid crossing your arms, legs, ankles, or wrists when talking to a customer. Crossing them suggests that you are closed to what the customer is saying; remaining open suggests that you are interested.

Watch your customers and try to gauge their moods through their body language.

Watch your customers and try to gauge their moods through their body language. Does the mother in the checkout line look tired and worn out? How can you provide service that will make her time with you as pleasant as possible? Something as simple as distracting her child for a moment while she pays for her purchase or offering to help her carry something could turn your time with her into a positive contact point for your organization.

Take a Moment

Have a coworker say the following items while frowning:

- "Our commitment is to top-quality service."

- "I'm glad you chose to do business with us today."

- "What can I do to help you?"

Now have them repeat the same messages with a smile. Listen and look at them. Are different messages communicated to the customer? Even when we are on the phone, customers can "hear" when we are smiling.

Tone of Voice

When you speak, customers listen to the tone you use as well as your words. Are you sincere? Do you show empathy and concern for their needs? A positive and caring tone says, "I understand how you feel. I'd be frustrated, too, if that happened to me." Here are some guidelines for using your voice effectively:

2

◆ Use a steady, moderate rate of speech. Speaking too fast could suggest to the customer that you are nervous or in a hurry; speaking too slowly could signal that you're bored.

◆ Never allow your voice to become overly loud or shrill. If a customer is yelling at you, you may be tempted to yell back, but don't. Maintaining a moderate volume and rate of speech can help calm an upset customer.

◆ Keep a smile in your voice. The smile on your face is reflected in the sound of your voice. Keep smiling, even if you're speaking on the phone. Your customers will hear the difference.

The smile on your face is reflected in the sound of your voice. Keep smiling, even if you're speaking on the phone.

◆ Increase the energy in your voice when speaking on the phone. The telephone can rob your voice of some of its natural expressiveness and energy, so be sure to compensate. And once again, smile; your customers can hear it.

The Right Words

As you work to create a positive impression through body language and tone of voice, don't discount the importance of the words you use. Choose positive words, even if your message is negative. When you cannot do what the customer wants, tell him or her what you will do for him rather than what you won't do.

◆ Instead of saying, "We don't have that in black," say, "We have that in gray, brown, and navy."

◆ Instead of saying, "I can't get that for you until Friday," say, "We'll have that for you on Friday. I'll call you if it comes in earlier."

♦ Instead of saying, "We don't give refunds," say, "I can offer you an exchange or credit toward a future purchase."

♦ Instead of saying, "May I help you?" or "Can I help you?" say, *"How* can I help you?"

The Cost of an Unhappy Customer

A lost customer is never just one sale, or even just one customer.

How important is treating your customer like a partner, having a positive attitude, and practicing good communication skills? Remember our statistics from Chapter 1—more customers leave an organization because of poor customer service than because of dissatisfaction with a product. And a lost customer is never just one sale, or even just one customer.

When you lose a customer, that customer tells 10 to 12 others, possibly building on the story each time. The unhappy customer tells people who might have been perfectly happy with you or planning on doing business with you in the future. Now, these other customers are not so sure, and your organization's future is not so bright.

But remember, customers don't want to be lost. They want to be delighted! And you have every opportunity to do just that. Your customers know what they want, when they want it, and how they want it—and that's the only thing they want. Listen to them, and do your best to meet their needs.

See your service through your customer's eyes. You can be clever, you can be smart, you can even be right; but none of that will matter to the customer unless your ultimate goal is to understand the problem, resolve the conflict, respond to the customer's concern, and make him or her feel better. This is the only way to give the kind of customer service that builds a positive total service experience for your customers.

> It doesn't matter whether customers are wrong or right; it matters how they feel when they hang up the phone.
>
> *Patti Wysocki*

Chapter Summary

As customers have more and more contacts with your organization, they combine their perceptions of those contacts into an overall impression of your organization's customer service. This impression is the customer's *total service experience.* The best way to ensure that customers remain loyal to your organization is to make sure that they have a positive total service experience. Some basic techniques that customer service stars use to create the best impression possible include:

2

◆ Treating your customer as a partner.

◆ Maintaining a positive attitude.

◆ Communicating effectively with your customer.

Following these guidelines will help you provide the kind of total service experience that will delight your customers and build a positive total service experience for them.

Self-Check: Chapter 2 Review

Answers to these questions appear on page 92.

1.   What is the *total service experience?*

   _____

   _____

2.   Who decides if a point of contact with your organization has been positive or negative?

   _____

   _____

3.   What two key questions will help you treat your customer as a partner?

   a. _____

   b. _____

4.   Positive self-talk will help you create a _____

   _____.

5.   True or false?
   Yelling at an upset customer is an effective way to get his or her attention and resolve the problem.

Chapter *Three*

Providing Service with Heart

Chapter Objectives

▶ Discuss how negative self-talk can interfere with positive customer relationships.

▶ Follow six steps for establishing an emotional connection with your customers.

▶ List the five steps of active listening.

Truly exceptional customer service is *service with heart*. When you give service with heart, you feel empathy for your customers, and your actions express your concern for them. Service with heart focuses on what the customer thinks, wants, and feels. Service with heart always puts the customer first.

Providing service with heart isn't always easy, even for service professionals. We are people, too, after all. We must deal with our moods, our emotions, and life's little distractions. We have both good days and bad days—and all these things affect our attitude. It's hard to be all smiles on the outside when you're worked up on the inside.

We can provide service with heart more consistently if we follow these three important guidelines:

◆ View all customers positively.

◆ Establish an emotional connection with your customers.

◆ Listen actively to all customer concerns.

Viewing Customers Positively

■ Roberto waited with dread as the next customer made her way to the customer service desk. The woman was frowning so sternly he thought her face might crack. "Oh, no," he said to himself as she plunked down her package on the counter. "It looks like I've got another fight on my hands."

You can't provide service with heart unless you maintain a positive attitude toward all your customers. In Chapter 2, we discussed self-talk and how it can help you develop a more positive attitude. Now let's look at how negative self-talk can have a detrimental effect on customer relationships.

Picture a challenging customer in your mind. If you usually work on the phone, hear his voice. If you wait on customers in person, watch her come through the door. What is your internal voice saying? Are you thinking, "On, no!" or "Not again!"? How do you think the rest of the transaction will go after that negative send-off? Negative self-talk interferes with your ability to develop an emotional connection with your customer.

On the other hand, how do you think your customer interactions would go if you engaged in positive self-talk about your customers? Let's return to our first example and see:

■ Roberto smiled with sympathy as the next customer made her way to the customer service desk. The woman looked tired, and she was carrying what looked like a very heavy package. "I'll bet it was a struggle for her to get her package down here today," he said to himself as she plunked down her package on the counter. "How can I help make this experience a little easier for her?"

Roberto's interaction in the second example will probably go much more smoothly than the first because he is going into the situation with a desire to help his customer.

Does it seem that certain members of your team always get the tough customers, the rude customers, or the "wrong" customers? Even if it appears to be true, it isn't. If someone else had handled that customer—someone with a different attitude—things probably would have turned out differently. A poor customer service attitude creates difficult customers. Listen to your self-

3

Negative self-talk interferes with your ability to develop an emotional connection with your customer.

33

talk for biases and prejudices. This can also affect how you serve some of your customers.

Your attitude toward your customer isn't the only thing that can affect your customer contacts. If some other aspect of your life is bothering you, it can affect the way you interact with your client, as in this example:

■ Bette was chronically ill and had spent many years in and out of health care facilities. Bette observed that the nurses some-times brought their problems to work. Although they gave polite and courteous service, they gave off what Bette referred to as "negative vibes." What Bette was "hearing" was reflected in their tone of voice and body language.

I am sure you have experienced "negative vibes" before—think about an experience in which a coworker or family member had a bad day. Did it destroy your good attitude to be around that person? Did you begin to wonder what you had done to upset him or her? The truth is that you probably didn't do anything. The other person became upset long before you encountered him or her; you were just hit with the fallout.

Service with heart requires an exceptional service attitude. Whether your negative thoughts are based in something that happened to you earlier that day or in negative expectations you have regarding a particular customer, replace them with these positive ones:

■ "I love helping customers."

■ "I'm eager to help."

■ "Problem solving is fun."

■ "I like connecting with customers."

■ "My customer is my partner. When she succeeds, I succeed."

Attitude is the reflection of a person, and our world mirrors our attitude.

Earl Nightingale

Your new attitude says, "Service with heart is what I give day in and day out." Positive self-talk and attitude influence the way we communicate.

Take a Moment

Jot down the answers to these questions after your next customer contact. Try it again two more times today.

1. How did you feel when you were dealing with your customer?

   _____

   _____

2. What was your attitude?

   _____

   _____

3. What emotions were affecting you from other parts of your life?

   _____

   _____

4. How did your internal dialogue affect the service you gave?

   _____

   _____

3

Building an Emotional Connection

Establishing an emotional connection with your customers is a key factor in providing service with heart. Begin by giving the customer your undivided attention. Then use these six strategies to build rapport.

◆ **Use the customer's name and title.** Learn your customer's name and title (Ms. Smith or Dr. Jones) and immediately begin using it. If the customer wants to be less formal and move to a first-name basis, follow her or his lead.

What if the customer's name is difficult to pronounce? Begin to pronounce the name, and the customer will usually help you. Repeat the name immediately after he or she says it to help you remember it. When you know you'll be working with the customer again, jot down a phonetic pronunciation of his or her name on an index card:

■ Mr. Grzanich (GRAZ-in-itch)
Ms. Sychra (see-CHAW-raw)

British Airways had all their employees use customers' names in every transaction for three months. At the end of the period, they surveyed their customers. Customer satisfaction rose 60 percent. Although using the customer's name probably wasn't the sole reason for the increase, their customers perceived British Airways as being more attentive. This made it easier to build rapport with customers.

◆ **Break the ice.** Think about how you connect with friends and coworkers every day. Use the same types of icebreakers with your customers. Here are some examples:

■ **Previous experience with products:** "I see that you tried our new inventory management software. How do you like it?"

■ **Common interests:** "How many rounds of golf have you gotten in this summer?"

■ **Recent events:** "Bob told me you just got back from vacation. How was the cruise?"

■ **Children and pets:** "You have a five-year-old? What a wonderful age—I remember when my son Aaron was that age."

Or the old standby—

■ **The weather:** "It's really been cold in your part of the country. Did that blackout affect your plant?"

When you are serving a repeat customer and have created a previous connection, use small talk or icebreakers to ease into a conversation and help you reestablish rapport. Keep to topics that are not offensive—and not too personal.

◆ **Avoid jargon.** If a word or phrase isn't common knowledge, or you wouldn't use it in everyday conversation with people outside your organization, don't use it with a customer. You understand what you're trying to say, but your words may confuse your customers, and they may be too embarrassed to ask for the meaning. If you must use an abbreviation or industry language, be ready to follow up with the definition. When you use vocabulary or jargon unfamiliar to customers, you risk failing to connect.

> If a word or phrase isn't common knowledge, don't use it with a customer.

3

Take a Moment

Jargon consists of words and phrases that are unique to your organization or industry, such as *download, ASAP, eighty-six,* and *stats.* By yourself or with members of your team, list all the abbreviations, words, and acronyms you use in your everyday contacts with the customer that could be classified as jargon. Provide the list to current and new employees.

_____

_____

_____

_____

◆ **Display confidence.** Customers will be more eager to work with you if they believe that you know what's going on. Instead of saying, "I don't know," say, "Let me get that information for you."

When we are not sure what to say, we often fill the silence with noise by saying *um, uh,* and *okay.* Your customer may become distracted by this filler noise and perceive it as showing a lack of confidence.

Remember that filler noise is different from the affirmations we give customers during active listening. Affirmations have a purpose—to assure the customer we are processing what she or he is saying. Fillers occupy empty space but add nothing meaningful to the conversation.

◆ **Show empathy.** When you are empathetic, you are sensitive to your customer's feelings and thoughts. Try to put yourself in your customers shoes, and solve the problem the way you would want it solved. In other words, follow the Golden Rule—treat others the way you would want to be treated. Here's an example of what happened when one customer service professional showed empathy for her customer:

■ One Memorial Day weekend, our neighbor Mary was having problems with her phone and needed to use ours. When she finished talking to the customer service representative, she was quite impressed by the service she had received. After Mary registered her complaint about the phone service, the representative said, "I apologize for your inconvenience, especially since this is your holiday weekend. I know this isn't something you wanted to deal with." After apologizing for the inconvenience caused by the poor telephone service, the representative began to collect the information she needed from Mary. She made an emotional connection with Mary through an empathetic statement before she began to solve Mary's problem.

Caution: Carefully choose your words when empathizing with a customer. Avoid blaming others or giving the customer too much information. When you share too much information, you run the risk of making the customer angrier. For instance, your customer does not need to know that 10 other customers called today with the same complaint. Instead, give a simple and sincere apology: "I'm sorry you were inconvenienced. I would have been frustrated if that happened to me."

◆ **Mirror the customer's speaking style and body language.** If your communication style is too different from your customer's style, you will not have credibility. This invites customers to think or say, "No, you don't understand." Matching your speaking style and body language to the customer's will help you connect with your customer.

If the customer is extremely friendly, show friendliness. If the customer sounds as if she is dealing with an emergency, show urgency. If the customer looks angry, show concern. Match the quality of your customers' emotions, *but never match their hostility or anger.*

> Getting people to like you is only the other side of liking them.
> *Norman Vincent Peale*

Actively Listening to Your Customers

3

Customers have needs beyond completing a simple business transaction—they have emotional needs as well. They need to feel welcome, important, valued, and understood. And there is no better or easier way to show your customers respect, concern, and understanding than by really listening to them.

An old saying states, "There's a difference between listening and waiting for your turn to talk." If you don't actively listen to your customers, you may assume that you know what they want, but you could be wrong. Don't conclude that you know what a customer wants after the first few sentences. You may need to ask for clarification before you fully understand the situation.

If you don't actively listen to your customers, you may assume that you know what they want, but you could be wrong.

Listening is not the same as hearing. *Hearing* is the physical act of processing sounds. *Active listening* means trying to find the real meaning of the words as well as the unspoken message behind them. In addition to the facts, you evaluate the speaker's tone of voice, body language, emotional state, and the context of the situation. Your goal is not just to hear words, but to understand the other person and let him or her know that you understand. That's how we let customers know we care, the essence of service with heart. Five guidelines that will help improve your active listening skills are listed on the next page.

Five Steps of Active Listening

1. **Be ready to listen.** Have paper and a pencil handy, or have your computer cleared and ready for the next customer contact.

2. **Be ready to take notes when appropriate.** If you are on the phone, let the customer know you are taking notes. Say, "I'm concerned about this, so I'm writing it down." When customers know you are taking notes, they are less likely to repeat themselves. This may also help them organize their thoughts.

3. **Show that you are listening.** If you are speaking to the customer in person, use your body language, stance, posture, and eye contact to show attentive silence. When talking on the phone, use attentive words, like "okay" or "I understand," to provide verbal reinforcement. This lets the customer know you are listening.

Your goal is to get the customer to talk to you.

4. **Ask questions.** Your goal is to get the customer to talk to you. Find out what he or she really wants. If things don't work out, help the customer vent some anger and frustration.

5. **Restate the customer's points.** Don't just repeat what the customer said—repeating is condescending and patronizing. Put the message in your own words, and don't restate the entire idea. Instead, emphasize the main points. Restating also invites corrections from the customer. This way you will know when you're on the right course.

Let's see how these guidelines work in the following case study:

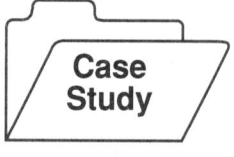

Case Study

■ Gary, your customer, has just called with a complaint about his order for Neon Sprockets. Gary placed his order a week ago and assumed he would have his merchandise by now. He is very concerned and more than a little irritated. Let's listen to Gary describe the situation:

Hello, this is Gary from Top-Notch Manufacturing. I placed a big order for Neon Sprockets last Wednesday, and I haven't heard anything from your company since. Don't you know I needed those sprockets yesterday? My production line is being held up because of you. Your salesman said he'd put a rush on this order. If this is your idea of a "rush," I can't believe you're still in business.

1. First, list the information you have so far:

    *   Customer's name: _____

    *   Customer's company: _____

    *   Product ordered: _____

    *   When product was ordered: _____

    *   Special instructions: _____

2. Next, follow through with this customer:

    *   **Empathize with Gary.** "I can understand why you're concerned. I'd be frustrated, too, if my production was being held up. I'm sorry for this delay."

    *   **Match his anger with urgency.** "I'll take immediate action on this."

    *   **Get the information you need.** "In order for me to confirm your order with our shipping department, I'll need some additional information. This will help us get our answer as quickly as possible."

    *   **Check on Gary's order with shipping.** If it is going to take more than a minute to get your answer, get Gary's phone number and tell him a specific time when you will call him back.

    *   **Follow through.** When you have the information from shipping, give Gary options—tell him what you can do for him. "Gary, your order has been filled and is ready to go out on today's truck. However, I talked to Tom in shipping, and we can run your sprockets over to the factory immediately. If this is acceptable, we'll have your order to you in two hours."

3

Note: Avoid phrases like "We'll put a rush on this," or "As soon as possible." Your interpretation of "rush" may differ from your customer's, causing confusion and misunderstandings. Instead, give the customer an exact time and date when the order will be delivered or when you will deal with a situation.

Your total communication, including your body language, tone of voice, and choice of words, will help you deal with situations like the case study above. But as important as your responses to your customers are, don't overlook the most important part of communication—listening. By listening attentively and making a real effort to understand your customer's concerns, you show the respect and understanding that are important parts of providing service with heart.

Take a Moment

How well do you listen?

To test yourself, tape-record your responses in customer service conversations over the course of the day.

1. At the end of the day, play back the tape, skipping the first 10 minutes (this is when you still remembered the tape was recording).

2. Notice the words you chose—were they positive or negative?

3. Did you listen more than you spoke?

Important: Save this tape for use in a later exercise.
If it is not practical for you to tape yourself, ask a coworker to monitor your actions. At the end of the day, ask the same questions.

Chapter Summary

Truly exceptional service is service with heart. Service with heart involves feeling empathy and concern for your customers; focusing on what the customer thinks, wants, and feels; and always putting the customer first.

You can provide service with heart more consistently if you view all customers positively. Engaging in positive self-talk will help you overcome negative attitudes and interact positively with your customers.

3

A key factor in providing service with heart is to establish an emotional connection with your customers. You can do this by:

- Using the customer's name and title.

- Building rapport with your customers.

- Avoiding jargon when you speak to customers.

- Displaying confidence to your customers.

- Showing empathy for your customers.

- Mirroring the customer's speech and body language.

Actively listening to customers is another important part of providing service with heart. You can listen more effectively to customers by:

- Being ready to listen.

- Being ready to take notes when appropriate.

- Showing your customer that you're listening.

- Asking questions.

- Restating the customer's points.

Self-Check: Chapter 3 Review

Answers to these questions appear on pages 92 and 93.

1. Service with heart focuses on what the customer

    _____, _____,

    and _____.

2. You can't provide service with heart unless you maintain a

    _____ _____ toward your
    customers.

3. What are three things you can do to build an emotional
    connection with your customers?

    a. _____

    b. _____

    c. _____

4. _____ is the physical act of processing

    sounds. _____ _____
    means trying to find the real meaning of the words and the
    unspoken message behind them.

5. The five steps of active listening are:

    a. _____

    b. _____

    c. _____

    d. _____

    e. _____

Chapter *Four*

Dealing with Challenging Customers

Chapter Objectives

▶ List four reasons why customers become upset.

▶ Identify your individual stress signals and use the S.T.O.P. method to remain calm.

▶ Establish ways to deal with the challenging, and sometimes angry, customer using a professional and capable approach.

Anyone can be nice to a nice customer. Dealing effectively with difficult customers is what separates the service professional from the mere amateur. Let's face it, some customers are going to be challenging. They're going to complain, get angry, and demand satisfaction on their terms. To understand why customers sometimes present these challenges, let's take a look at the roots of customer dissatisfaction.

Why Customers Get Upset

Although there are many different reasons why customers may become dissatisfied, they generally have one thing in common: the perceived value of your product or service was less than the customer expected. Here are four shortcomings that can cause a customer to view your product or service negatively:

◆ **The customer didn't get what was promised or what was expected.** To overcome this, you must raise the quality of the product, or in some cases, work to make the customer's expectations more realistic.

- **Someone was rude to the customer.** Whether the employee knew it or not, this was the customer's perception.

- **Someone was indifferent to the customer.** An employee projected a "can't-do" attitude.

- **No one listened to the customer.** Of all four reasons, this is the most troubling. Failing to listen to a customer is a tragic waste of an opportunity for the feedback your organization needs to improve processes, products, or services.

4

Take a Moment

Try to recall the last time you complained about a product or service. Did your complaint fall into one of the categories just described? If so, which one? If not, how would you describe the nature of your complaint?

_____

_____

_____

Each problem has hidden in it an opportunity so powerful that it literally dwarfs the problem. The greatest success stories were created by people who recognized a problem and turned it into an opportunity.

Joseph Sugarman

Dealing with Customer Emotions

When customers are dissatisfied, they can become difficult, frustrated, and quick to anger. What you as a service professional must realize is that an angry customer doesn't respond to logic. In fact, the more logical you are, the angrier the customer will probably become. No matter what you say and no matter how you phrase it, you simply will not be able to penetrate the customer's emotional barrier. Stating, "Now just calm down," will only escalate the customer's anger. Before you can work on the customer's problem, you need to deal with the customer's emotions.

An angry customer doesn't respond to logic.

Calming Yourself

To calm an angry customer, you must stay calm yourself.

To calm an angry customer, you must stay calm yourself. Relaxation techniques can help, but this is easier said than done. Try to keep your voice open and relaxed. When you hear your voice sounding rushed or panicked, take a few deep breaths and use positive self-talk to help you gain composure. Say, "I can handle this. I am in control."

Use the S.T.O.P. method to help you deal with stressful situations. S.T.O.P. stands for:

◆ Signal

◆ Take Control

◆ Opposite

◆ Practice

◆ **Signal**
Look for your own early warning signals of stress. Do you clench your jaws? Does your heart pound? Does tension build in your neck and shoulders? Does your temperature rise and your face flush? Any of these are signs that you are feeling anxious. If you aren't sure what your signal is, ask your coworkers or family. Children are especially good at identifying stress signals.

◆ **Take control**
After you have identified your early-warning signals, you can take control of your own mind and body.

◆ **Opposite**
Do the opposite of your early-warning signal. If your jaw is clenched, relax your face muscles. If your pulse is racing, breathe slowly and deeply. If you feel yourself overheating, drink something cool (not cold) or lukewarm. The act of swallowing will also help relax your throat muscles and relieve a dry mouth.

◆ **Practice**
Practice these actions whenever you feel tense, whether at work, on the drive home during rush hour, or during a family emergency.

Take a Moment

What are your stress signals? What actions can you take that are opposite to those stress signals?

_____

_____

Calming the Upset Customer

Once your emotions are under control, turn your attention to calming your customer by following these steps:

1. **Remain calm yourself.** Do not react emotionally, no matter how upset the customer gets.

2. **Let the customer vent.** Actively listen and let the customer know you are listening.

   ◆ Don't interrupt. Have you ever been so angry that you practiced what you were going to say? The customer is no different. The customer has a list of items to cover, and if you interrupt, she or he will just start at the beginning again.

   ◆ Wait until the venting finishes. You might hear a sigh or sense that the customer is winding down. Avoid saying, "Are you finished yet?" It will do nothing to improve the situation. Be patient. Although you may be tempted to give the customer a solution to the problem, he or she is not yet ready to hear it.

3. **Deal with emotions first.** You must resolve the customer's emotions before you can begin to solve his or her problem. Acknowledging the customer's emotions makes the customer feel valued and allows you to develop a partnership with the customer. This partnership is the foundation for the problem-solving task you are about to begin. There are three ways to acknowledge your customer's emotions:

   ◆ Restate what customer said. By paraphrasing, you let the customer know you heard and give the customer the opportunity to clarify her or his concerns.

You must resolve the customer's emotions before you can begin to solve his or her problem.

4

◆ Show empathy. When you show empathy, you show concern. This is not the same as agreement. Statements such as "I can understand why you feel that way," or "I'd be upset if that happened to me," allow you to empathize with the customer but do not place blame on anyone in your organization.

◆ Find agreement. When you find agreement, you clearly identify the real problem, and working in partnership, you get on the same side as the customer. The enemy is now the problem, not you.

4. **Thank the customer for bringing the problem to your attention.**

5. **Avoid emotional trigger phrases.** When you use a *trigger* or *"no" phrase,* you run the risk of damaging an already fragile relationship. If you've done everything right so far in the damage-control area, the use of calming or "yes" phrases further strengthens the partnership you have developed with the customer. Use calming phrases to describe what you can do for the customer to solve his or her problem.

Trigger Phrases	Calming Phrases
Policy	Here's what we can do . . . ; Here's how we can handle this . . . (quote the policy, just don't call it "policy")
Can't	Can
Sorry	Thank you
No/I don't know	I can find out
But	And
You should have	Let's do this (move to the future, not the past)
Why didn't you	I can see why
The only thing we can do	The best option, I think

6. **Set limits with abusive customers.** In rare circumstances, you will have a customer who is loud or abusive, or cannot be calmed down. In this case, gently set limits with the abusive customer.

   ◆ If you know the customer's name, use it.

   ◆ Use a sympathetic tone of voice to request the customer's cooperation and include a help statement.

   ■ Example: "Mr. Young, I really want to help you. I am finding it difficult as long as you continue to use this language. I can help you resolve this. Will you let me help you?"

   This type of statement clearly and respectfully communicates your desire to help if the customer will let you.

4

7. **As a last resort, delay action or seek a second opinion.** By delaying action, you give yourself and the customer a needed time-out. You also show the customer that you're taking his cause to a higher level. This alone may have a calming effect on the customer.

   ◆ Get back to the customer as promised. If necessary, bring your manager or supervisor in on the conversation.

An angry customer will remember that you handled a complaint with poise and professionalism long after she or he forgets what the complaint was about. At any time during this process, when the customer has calmed down, move to problem solving. After all, solving the customer's problem is, and always has been, your final goal.

> An angry customer will remember that you handled a complaint with poise and professionalism long after she or he forgets what the complaint was about.

Take a Moment

Listen again to the audiotape you made for the exercise on page 42, and identify any trigger words or phrases. Make a mark next to the following words and phrases each time they occur:

Policy _____

Can't _____

Sorry _____

I don't know _____

But . . . _____

You should have _____

Why didn't you _____

The only thing we can do _____

Practice substituting a calming phrase in place of any trigger phrases you currently use. Make a list of calming statements and post it next to your desk.

Chapter Summary

Dealing effectively with difficult customers is the mark of the true customer service professional. Customers who become challenging are often dissatisfied because they perceive the value of your product or service as being less than they expected.

Before you can solve the customer's problem, you must help the customer deal with his or her emotions. You can do this by following these steps:

◆ Remain calm yourself.

◆ Let the customer vent.

◆ Acknowledge the customer's emotions.

◆ Thank the customer for bringing the problem to your attention.

◆ Avoid emotional trigger phrases.

◆ Set limits with abusive customers.

◆ Delay action or seek a second opinion as a last resort.

4

Self-Check: Chapter 4 Review

Answers to these questions appear on page 93.

1. Four shortcomings that can cause a customer to view your product or service negatively are:

   a. _____

   b. _____

   c. _____

   d. _____

2. True or false?
   Saying to a customer, "Just calm down now," is a more effective way to handle an emotional outburst than simply allowing the customer to vent his or her feelings.

3. True or false?
   Before you can begin to deal with a challenging customer, you must have your own emotions under control.

4. What do the letters of the S.T.O.P. method for handling stress stand for?

   _____

   _____

   _____

   _____

5. Acknowledging a customer's emotions helps a customer feel

   _____ and allows you to

   _____ _____

   _____ with the customer.

Chapter *Five*

Solving Customer Problems

Chapter Objectives

▶ Build realistic expectations for customers.

▶ Involve customers in the problem-solving process.

▶ Provide customers with alternatives when delivering bad news.

Solving problems for customers is one of the primary goals of a customer service professional. When we think of problem solving, we generally think of solving problems after they arise—a sort of crisis management. This is the *traditional view* of problem solving. But to exceed customers' expectations and provide exceptional service, you and your organization must try to anticipate problems and solve them before they start. This is *proactive problem solving.* You can begin your proactive approach to problem solving by following these steps:

♦ Manage customer expectations.

♦ Quickly solve problems that do arise.

♦ Work cooperatively with customers who are wrong.

♦ Deliver bad news effectively.

Managing Customer Expectations

The first step in proactive problem solving is to build realistic expectations for your customers. As we saw in Chapter 4, customers become disappointed when they do not get what they expected. These expectations may not be sound from your organization's standpoint, but that doesn't make them any less real to your customers. Their dissatisfaction creates the problems you have to solve.

You can help customers maintain realistic expectations by following this simple rule: *never overpromise, and never oversell.* Let customers know exactly how your product or service will perform under general conditions at the original point of sale or service. Help customers understand what they can realistically expect from your organization.

> **Never overpromise, and never oversell.**

As you work with your customers, try to anticipate any problems that could arise with your product or service. Tell customers about these potential problems before they arise; educate and inform them. Discuss extra costs or possible delays. Some examples of statements you might make include:

- "This model isn't designed to handle extreme temperatures. For that, you should consider our other model."

- "The special features you requested will involve some additional charges beyond our base price."

- "Your order will take three days to deliver instead of our usual two."

- "It will take us three weeks to process your claim forms."

Keep the customer informed by staying in touch on a regular basis.

5

Take a Moment

What does your company currently do to help customers develop realistic expectations regarding your product or service? Are there other things you could do to help avoid future complaints? List them below.

_____

_____

_____

_____

_____

Solving Problems When They Arise

Even though you try to anticipate problems and solve them before they begin, there will be times when your product or service doesn't perform as promised, and a customer is disappointed. This is a crucial moment in your organization's relationship with that customer. Remember our figures from Chapter 2—if customers believe you are responsive to a problem, they will do business with your organization again 82 to 95 percent of the time. Those customers will also become your organization's most effective advertisement as they tell their friends about the incredible customer service they received.

To help your customer reach a satisfactory solution to his or her problem, follow these steps:

1. **Thank the customer for bringing the problem to your attention.** By taking the time to complain, the customer is giving you the chance to restore his or her relationship with your organization.

2. **Listen and gather information.** Give the customer a chance to discuss the problem and vent her or his emotions. Be sure to get the customer's name, address, and phone number and record the specifics of the complaint.

3. **Apologize sincerely for the problem.** Customers can tell whether a customer service representative sincerely wants to help them or is just faking it.

4. **Take responsibility for fixing the problem.** Don't blame others or make excuses.

> Involve the customer in the solution. Do what is most useful to the customer, not easiest for you.

5. **Involve the customer in the solution.** This is the most important step in problem solving. Do what is most useful to the customer, not easiest for you. Ask, "How would you like us to handle this?"

6. **Solve the problem quickly.** Give the customer this message through your actions: "What happened to you was unusual. What happened to you was a fluke. This is what's normal." Your customer wants a resolution to the problem, and he or she will be delighted if you act quickly to resolve it.

7. **Do something extra.** What sets exceptional customer service apart from traditional customer service is the realization that correcting the problem is just not enough. This is your organization's opportunity to say, "We're sorry we wasted your time, energy, and money. The only reason this problem occurred is because our organization didn't do something right the first time." An extra might include giving a customer a gift certificate for a meal, a free pass to a movie or sporting event, or crediting a customer's account for a future order.

8. **Ask for repeat business.** Ask the customer to give your company a second chance. In sales terms, close the sale—ask for the repeat business: "We hope we'll have the chance to serve you again."

9. **Follow up.** Forward the details about the problem to the appropriate department within your organization for correction. Send the customer a written follow-up. If appropriate, tell the customer what actions you have taken to correct the system, product, or service.

5

Take a Moment

Think about the last time you solved a problem for a customer. Did you follow the steps just discussed? Now that you are familiar with these steps, what would you have done differently?

_____

_____

_____

Dealing with the Customer Who Is Wrong

You've probably heard the saying, "The customer is always right." Yet in reality, you can think of circumstances in which the customer has not been right. Usually when this happens, the customer has different expectations than you had hoped he or she might have. Perhaps the customer was promised too

Customers may not always be right, but they are always customers.

much by an overeager employee, or the customer assumed you provided a specific service as standard. When this happens, remember—customers may not always be right, but they are always customers. Here are some techniques to use when a customer is wrong:

♦ **Thank the customer for the complaint.**

♦ **Deal with emotions first.** Help the customer express dissatisfaction and empathize with him or her.

♦ **Establish the facts.** Get the customer's understanding of the situation. Use the active-listening skills discussed in Chapter 3. Accept what the customer tells you. Don't discount what the customer says; that's as good as saying he or she is a liar.

♦ **Maintain respect.** Do not place blame on the customer.

♦ **Move to problem solving.** A common approach is to look for a company policy that supports your position. Instead, I would recommend looking for a way to help the customer. Explain your organization's position without referring to policies or anything that smacks of red tape. If you're not sure what you can do or need additional time to weigh options, say, "Let me check into this and get back to you."

♦ **Find the best available option.** Try to be flexible. If possible, let the customer be right. If that isn't possible, tell the customer what you *can* do instead of what you *can't* do.

The following example shows the way one bank representative helped a customer who was wrong:

■ A customer calls the bank to complain about her monthly service charge. Her account balance has gone below a certain minimum amount, and a fee is assessed by the bank. When the customer calls, the representative says, "I'm sorry you are surprised by this charge. It's customary for customers to be told about this service charge when they open their accounts. I'll remove the charge from your account this month, and I'll make a note in your account that we have reviewed this information."

The bank representative gave the customer what she wanted—the removal of the service fee (at least for this month)—and gently educated her that a fee would be assessed each time the balance fell below the minimum amount. She also told the customer that she is documenting their conversation so there will be less opportunity for misunderstanding in the future.

Take a Moment

Francesca has just taken a call from her customer, Mr. Wong. Mr. Wong believed that his new office copier came with a service agreement. In reality, the service agreement must be purchased in addition to the copier. Mr. Wong is angry after receiving his first bill for the repair of the copier. Francesca responds:

■ Thank you for bringing this to our attention, Mr. Wong. I can see why you might believe you would receive a service plan with your copier. I think our best option is to remove the fee for the labor and charge you only for the parts for the June 18 service call. Even with a service agreement, you would be charged for the parts. I'll also send you a packet outlining our service options. We have some reasonably priced packages, or we can customize a package to meet your needs. Would you prefer to have a sales representative stop by your office next week to answer your questions, or would you rather I called and discussed your options?

Notice how Francesca never tells Mr. Wong "no." Instead, Francesca finds several ways to tell him "yes." Find the places in the case study where Francesca does the following:

1. Thanks the customer.

2. Empathizes with the customer.

3. Reviews alternatives and offers the best solution.

4. Educates and informs the customer.

5. Arranges for follow-up.

Answers appear on pages 93 and 94.

5

Delivering Bad News

There will come a time when you must deliver bad news to a customer. You may have to tell the customer that you won't take something back, the item ordered is out of stock, or you need payment in advance.

Here are some suggestions for delivering bad news:

Inform the customer of bad news as early in the process as possible.

1. **Look for an alternative first.** If no alternatives exist, proceed with the remaining steps.

2. **Inform the customer as early in the process as possible.**

3. **Inform the customer over the phone or in person, not by letter.**

4. **Get to the point quickly.** You can warn the customer that bad news is coming by saying something like "You're not going to like hearing this, but . . ." This can soften the news.

5. **Treat the customer fairly.** Your courtesy and professionalism will be remembered long after the actual problem is forgotten.

Here's how one customer service representative made bad news easier to deal with:

■ Liz is a customer service representative for a company that provides products for other businesses, such as safety equipment, nameplates, and recycling bins. She took an order from a new customer and told the customer when he would receive his order. However, when Liz turned the order in, the credit department required 50 percent of the payment in advance before the order could be started. This took a few days to resolve, which held up the order, jeopardizing the initial delivery date. The customer was not happy. Not only did he have to prepay, but his order was being held up.

By taking the extra effort to work closely with production, Liz made sure the order was delivered on the original date promised. When the order was delivered, Liz had it sent by courier, sent a personal letter of apology, and enclosed a pen and pencil set (something extra to offset the customer's inconvenience). Liz exceeded the customer's expectations, and sure enough, the customer ordered from the company again.

When You Can't Satisfy a Customer

You probably have dealt with customers that you could not satisfy, no matter how hard you tried. When nothing seems to satisfy the customer, take these additional steps:

1. **Sincerely apologize that you are unable to help the customer.**

2. **Ask for a chance in the future.** There is always an opportunity to restore the relationship.

3. **Do *not* let this contact affect your contact with the next customer.**

Despite difficult and demanding customers, most customer service professionals agree that one of the most rewarding facets of the job is taking a customer who is having a bad day or a bad experience and turning that customer's experience around.

Talking with the Boss

Even the most experienced customer service professionals have customers who will only be satisfied by talking to a superior. When the customer demands to talk with the manager, the owner, or the president of your organization:

1. **Ask for information so you can transfer the customer.** Say, "So that I can direct your call to the right person, can you tell me what this concerns?" Notice that this statement acknowledges the customer's request.

2. **After the customer gives you the information, offer to handle the situation for the customer yourself if you are able.** Reassure the customer that you can handle the situation by saying something like "Oh, that's an issue I can answer right away for you." If the customer still wishes to talk to your manager, follow through with the request.

3. **Transfer the call when necessary—but only after collecting information and explaining the situation to your manager.** Make sure that you tell the manager everything, including:

    ◆ The customer's name.

    ◆ The problem.

5

◆ What has been done up to this point.

Don't leave anything out! If by some chance you've made an error or given the customer inaccurate information, tell your supervisor. This is not the time to hold anything back.

Your company can initiate changes that reduce the number of times a supervisor must intercede. Many progressive companies give customer service professionals the authority to refund money up to a certain dollar amount, drop shipping charges, or credit accounts for future orders. These are just a few ways an organization encourages exceptional customer relations.
One hotel chain allows any employee, from a member of the housekeeping staff to the hotel manager, up to $1,000 to resolve situations with customers. If you believe changes such as these would benefit your organization, offer suggestions to your manager. After all, a customer service professional is always looking for ways to make the customer's experience a more positive one.

> **Your company can initiate changes that reduce the number of times a supervisor must intercede.**

Chapter Summary

To exceed customers' expectations and provide exceptional service, you and your organization must try to anticipate problems and solve them before they start. This is *proactive problem solving.* The first step in proactive problem solving is to build realistic expectations for your customers. This can help you avoid customer dissatisfaction with your product.

When customers are dissatisfied, you need to provide quick solutions to their problems. Involve the customer in the problem-solving process—do what is most useful for the customer, not what is easiest for you. When a dissatisfied customer is wrong, gently explain your company's position without referring to policies or red tape. Stress what you *can* do for your customer rather than what you *can't* do.

If you discover that some aspect of a situation will disappoint a customer, let the customer know as early in the process as possible, and do as much as you can to make the bad news easier to deal with. If you find that you absolutely cannot satisfy a customer, apologize that your were not able to help and ask for a chance to serve him or her again in the future.

Self-Check: Chapter 5 Review

Answers to these questions appear on page 94.

1. When we try to anticipate problems and solve them before they start, we are taking a _____ approach to problem solving.

2. Building expectations in your customers can help you avoid the customer _____ that leads to complaints.

3. True or false?
   When trying to solve a problem, you have a responsibility to choose the solution that will be easiest for your company to handle, whether it is the best solution for the customer or not.

4. True or false?
   If a customer asks to speak to your supervisor, you should turn that person over to him or her immediately so as not to waste time.

5. True or false?
   When you are unable to satisfy a customer, the best approach is to apologize sincerely and ask for a chance to serve him or her in the future.

5

Chapter *Six*

Helping Customers over the Phone

> ## Chapter Objectives
>
> ▶ Use the one-voice concept to help customers feel in control during calls.
>
> ▶ Use six tactics for transferring calls effectively.
>
> ▶ Follow four steps for putting a caller on hold.

Many customer service professionals spend a good deal of their time dealing with customers over the telephone. Telephone customer service has its own special challenges. Customers often feel a loss of control when they are dealing with a company over the telephone. (How many times have you called an organization and been cut off or lost in the voice-mail system?) As a representative of your company, it's your job to provide customers with the same type of caring service they would receive if they visited you in person.

Providing One Voice for Your Customers

Customers are going to be much more satisfied if they are handled by the first person they talk to.

One of the best ways to deliver exceptional telephone service is to master the one-voice technique. Customers want to identify with you as the voice of your organization, and they want to feel that sense of responsiveness that is part of service with heart. With this in mind, customers are going to be much more satisfied if they are handled by the first person they talk to, without having to explain their situation over and over again. By being the sole contact with the customer, you form an important partnership.

Whenever possible, try to avoid transferring customers. If you can identify a set of questions that customers regularly ask, have those answers available at your desk so you'll be ready when customers call. If possible, offer to get the answer to your customer's question yourself and call him or her back.

Take a Moment

How many times each day do you transfer callers? What actions can you take that would allow you to handle more calls yourself instead of transferring them? Write the answers below.

_____

_____

_____

_____

Transferring the Customer

6

In order to provide the best service for your customers, you will sometimes have to transfer them to another person or department. Unfortunately, this is something customers usually don't like. In order to keep them from feeling that they are getting the runaround, keep them informed, and let them know you're not just passing the buck.

When you do have to transfer a call, keep these tactics in mind:

1. **State what you *can* do, not what you *can't* do.** Turn a negative into a positive by letting customers know you are acting for their benefit: "I can help you by letting you talk to someone in accounts receivable."

2. **Avoid using the word *transfer.*** Customers don't like this word. Instead say, "Let me connect you to . . . ," "I'll let you talk with . . . ," or "Let me put you in touch with . . ." Again, communicate the benefits of your actions clearly to the customer.

> **When you need to transfer a customer, state what you *can* do, not what you *can't* do.**

3. **Pass along customer information.** When transferring a call, pass along the customer's name and any facts you have obtained so far. This will make customers feel that they're making progress since they don't have to repeat their information.

4. **Stay on the line.** Introduce the customer to the next employee if possible. And never transfer a call if you are not completely sure the next employee is available to take it. Although voice mail has grown increasingly popular, do not assume your customer will be satisfied with leaving a message.

5. **Follow up.** Before transferring a customer's call, ask for the customer's phone number. If you accidentally cut the customer off in the process, call him or her back.

6. **If you're uncertain to whom to transfer a call, don't guess.** Collect as much information as you can from the caller, and tell the caller that you will get back to her or him. Then call around your company, get the solution or information the customer needs, and call back. If another employee is going to call your customer back, make sure that employee follows through.

> Before transferring a customer's call, ask for the customer's phone number.

What If the Customer Asks Not to Be Transferred?

Sometimes the customer will ask not to be transferred. Likewise, if you are the third person your customer has talked to, do not transfer him, even if you're not the person to whom he needs to speak. Stay with the customer, find out whatever you can about the situation, and agree on a time when you will call the customer back. Then do the research yourself and call the customer with the information.

When the Call Is Transferred to You

If you're the employee that the call is being forwarded to, how do you help the customer feel important? First of all, identify yourself. Then let the customer know you are aware of her situation. Say, "Hello, this is Lisa. Mrs. Brown, I understand you have a question about the 30-day grace period. I have your account information in front of me and I can help you with that." That way the customer doesn't have to repeat herself. Her mental image is that progress is being made.

Take a Moment

The telephone is a tool that most organizations can't function without. Yet many people don't know how to use their phones to the fullest. If your phone has buttons, functions, or abilities that you don't understand, get training right away. Go to the people in your company who do know how to use the phone and ask for their help.

Using the Hold Button

If customers don't like the idea of being transferred, they certainly don't like the idea of being put on hold. By pushing your hold button a little too quickly or a little too often, you can easily damage your relationships with your customers.

Your best solution is to not put the customer on hold at all. Why appear to waste their time? You may want to say, "May I have a number where I can reach you? I'll call you back in 10 minutes, and I'll have that information for you." After 10 minutes, whether you have that information or not, call the customer.

6

Four Crucial Steps for Putting a Customer Call on Hold

If you find you must put the customer on hold, follow these steps:

1. Ask permission.

    ◆ Always ask, "Will you hold, please?"

    ◆ Wait for a response. There is nothing more annoying than being asked and then hearing the phone click to hold before you've had time to respond.

2. Get back to the customer after no more than 45 seconds.

    ◆ Shoot for a maximum of 30 seconds. Never go beyond 45 seconds without coming back on the line for an update.

3. Thank the customer for holding.

    ◆ Always say, "Thanks for holding."

    ◆ Do not say, "I'm sorry you had to hold." This invites the response, "You should be sorry. Every time I call your company I'm put on hold."

4. Offer to call back instead of putting the customer on hold.

    ◆ If you know the process is going to take a little extra time, offer to call the customer back within a certain time frame.

Chapter Summary

Customers often feel powerless when they are on the phone. Using the one-voice technique creates a connection with your customers that gives them a sense of control and brings humanity to your transaction. When you do need to transfer customers or put them on hold, always let them know that you are doing so in order to provide them with better service. Through hard work and practice, you can maximize your customer service effectiveness both in person and on the phone.

Self-Check: Chapter 6 Review

Discussion of answers appears on pages 94 and 95.

1. How would you rate your telephone customer service skills?
    Poor   Fair   Good   Excellent

2. How many times during the day do you transfer customers?
    4–5   6–10   11–20   20+

3. How many times during the day are calls transferred to you?
    4–5   6–10   11–20   20+

4. How many times will a customer be transferred?
    1   2   3   4 or more

5. How many customers per day do you put on hold?
    1–5   6–10   11–20   20+

6. How many seconds does the on-hold period usually last?
    1–15   16–30   31–45   45+

7. a. Do you ask if you can put the customer on hold?
        Yes   No
    b. Do you always wait for a response?
        Yes   No

6

8. Say aloud your standard phone greeting. Is it recognizable as
    more than one word, or do you run the words together?

Chapter *Seven*

Becoming a Customer Service Star

> ## Chapter Objectives
>
> ▶ Determine what traits customer service stars have in common.
>
> ▶ Improve your attitude toward customers and life by practicing survival skills.

We all have customer service stars in our organizations. These stars have an intense desire to exceed their customers' expectations. They want the customer to walk away dazzled. Stars set the standard for customer service in any organization. But stars weren't born to excel—they worked to develop their customer service skills, and they continue to improve them every day. This means that anyone can become a star by taking on the challenge of being exceptional.

What Makes a Customer Service Star?

It's one thing to talk about becoming a customer service star, and another to put the customer service principles into action. Let's look at some characteristics customer service stars share that make them similar. Customer service stars:

◆ Become internally motivated to serve.

◆ Convey a sincere interest in others.

◆ Maintain a positive attitude.

◆ Remain energized and enthusiastic.

◆ Know their organizations inside and out.

◆ Track their own performance.

◆ Take initiative.

Let's take a closer look at these attributes and think how you can enhance your customer service skills and become a customer service star.

> Our beliefs about what we are and what we can be precisely determine what we will be.
>
> *Anthony Robbins*

Becoming Internally Motivated to Serve

People are not motivated by external sources. Motivation can only come from inside a person. Customer service stars maintain their motivation to exceed their customer's expectations. They gain personal satisfaction from dazzling the customer and leaving the customer feeling better than when the customer started the interaction.

> **People are not motivated by external sources. Motivation can only come from inside a person.**

Take a Moment

The next time you have an especially successful customer service contact, pay special attention to how you feel. Let this positive feeling become your motivation as you strive to make all your customer contacts equally successful.

Conveying a Sincere Interest in Others

Service stars are genuinely interested in their customers, and they let customers know it by remaining flexible and adapting to meet their needs. Stars try to understand what makes their customers tick—they search for the key to each customer's satisfaction. They put preconceived biases and judgments aside, as in this example.

■ My friend Bob sells BMW automobiles. One day, a casually dressed individual pulled in to the dealership in an old pickup truck. It was cold and rainy, and the salespeople debated on who had to go out and help this unlikely customer. Finally, Bob volunteered. Bob learned that this man owned a large carpet business, and he had come to the dealership straight from the plant. His other car, a BMW, had been stolen the week before. Bob sold his customer a $60,000 car that day.

7

73

Who knows who your best customers might be? A service superstar realizes that every customer, no matter how unlikely, is important.

Maintaining a Positive Attitude

When you feel positive, it's easier to communicate with customers. Stars expect things to work out. They feel positive about their work and their lives, and they convey that attitude to the customer through their body language, tone of voice, and of course, their words. Customers can feel their positive energy, and they come away feeling positive too.

Remaining Energized and Enthusiastic

If you live enthusiastically every day, you will remain energized, and your whole outlook will improve.

One of the greatest things you can do for yourself is to get excited about your work and your life. If you live enthusiastically every day, you will remain energized, and your whole outlook will improve. If you wait for some lucky event to occur before you get energized, you will be waiting a long time for an exciting life.

True customer service stars are sincere in their energy and enthusiasm. A customer knows when you're faking it; customers can detect falseness and insincerity. Take a look at the following example of sincere enthusiasm.

■ My day had started in a small town in western New York. I had driven two hours to the airport in Buffalo, flown to Albany, and had just started another drive to reach a conference in New Paltz, New York. I took the exit off the interstate and pulled into a tollbooth.

I paid the tollbooth attendant and began searching for my directions to the hotel. Without any prompting, the attendant asked, "Do you need some help with directions?" When I answered "Yes" and told him where I was going, he replied, "You're at the right exit. Have you ever been here before?" I answered "No."

"You have just entered one of the prettiest places in the United States—the Hudson River Valley," he said. After giving me directions and warning about deer on the road, he finished with, "This place is beautiful. You're going to love it." This tollbooth attendant turned my day around. His contagious enthusiasm for the area impressed me and excited me about the drive—and his description was right. My long, tiring day had been transformed by my encounter with this service star.

Getting to Know Your Organization

Service stars have an unstoppable sense of curiosity. Stars not only learn their own jobs and departments, but they also learn about other departments as well. They try to see the big picture for the customer. This awareness helps them serve the customer better. They keep up-to-date on new product lines, product upgrades, specials, sales, and incentives.

Service stars try to see the big picture.

Take a Moment

Are there areas of your company that you know little about? What can you do in the next week to learn more about them? Write an action plan below.

_____

_____

_____

Tracking Your Performance

Most of us want to hear positive feedback, but customer service stars want both positive and corrective feedback. They think of corrective feedback as being constructive and informative.

Corrective feedback provides you with the information you need to better serve your customers. It is not the same as criticism, which implies judgment. Try to view all customer feedback as a gift that will help you improve your performance.

When customers provide you with corrective feedback, make a note of it. If there is something you can do to change the situation, develop a plan for doing it. If the feedback relates to something over which you have no control, pass it along to the appropriate person or team.

Invite customer feedback whenever possible. This can be as simple as asking customers what they think about a certain product or service, or more formal, such as asking them to fill out a response card or take part in a focus group. If your organization has no program for encouraging customer feedback, suggest that it start one.

7

Customer feedback can also provide your company with valuable information. Your customers are your organization's best source of marketing information. As a service professional, you are the link between your customer and the company.

Taking Initiative

To take *initiative* means to take *action*. Many organizations empower their service professionals to do whatever it takes to satisfy the customer. The organization establishes guidelines, but after that it's up to the service representative. Unfortunately, sometimes people have been trained, educated, and empowered— and they do nothing. A customer service star is ready and willing to act. Use whatever power you have been given on behalf of your customers.

Keeping Your Attitude Up All Day Long

A true service star maintains these characteristics all day long, despite the stress and pressure that come with the job. How can you be consistently nice to, concerned about, and interested in a customer, and then do the same thing over and over, day after day? Here are some survival techniques that will help you do just that.

1. **Remind yourself to engage in positive self-talk.** Practice healthy thinking. Don't clutter your mind with negatives.

2. **Get a calming object.** Choose something from your past (memories), or something for your future (goals and plans). Use a photo, cartoon, or positive notes that remind you that this too shall pass. My friend Carla has the saying "They say you can't do it, but sometimes that doesn't always work" taped to her computer. It reminds her that there are solutions for seemingly impossible situations.

3. **Focus on successes rather than negatives.** Track the things that go right. Go to the "Take a Moment" exercise on page 78 for a fun and easy way to track your customer successes.

4. **Use your break effectively.** Do something to keep yourself going. Relax and clear your mind. Listen to music, play motivational or inspirational tapes, take a walk, or read. Don't use your free time for complaining.

5. **Develop a buddy system.** Learn from each other, and share the load. Work with your coworkers to give each other breaks from stress.

6. **Take care of yourself.** When the details are getting you down, step back and look at the big picture. Exercise, volunteer, spend time with friends and family, and do other things that add value to your life.

7. **Bring your sense of humor to work.** Take your work seriously, but don't take yourself seriously. Learn to laugh at yourself, and don't forget to take your sense of humor back home with you. Your spouse, your children, and even your pets will appreciate it.

Take a Moment

Within your team or group, list the different ways members keep a positive attitude, such as:

1. Listening to music on break

2. Keeping family photos nearby

3. Walking or exercising over lunch

4. _____

5. _____

6. _____

When you have a solid list, select one item that you do not currently do and give it a try for the next week. The following week, try another one. This will give you additional ways to keep your attitude strong and positive all day long.

7

Can you be a customer service star? Evaluate where you are today. If you are truly unhappy in your work, maybe you're in the wrong job. But if you basically like your work and just feel the need for a few changes, the best place to start may be to change yourself.

Think positively. Develop a feeling of concern for your customers. Keep a sense of humor. Before you know it, you'll see yourself as a customer service star, and so will everyone around you.

Take a Moment

If you are having trouble focusing on positive customer experiences, try this trick to get an accurate reading on the number of positive and negative experiences you encounter every day. On a piece of paper, write the words "Start" and "End," and place a plus and a minus sign under each word. "Start" shows whether a customer is in a positive or negative mood when you start your interaction. "End" shows whether the customer has a positive or negative attitude at the end of the conversation. Place check marks in the total column to indicate how you did. I'm sure you will find that you have many more positive endings than negative ones.

	Customer Mood		
	Start	End	Total
Customer began positive, ended positive	+	+	✓✓✓✓
Customer began negative, ended negative	-	-	✓✓
Customer began negative, ended positive	-	+	✓✓✓
Customer began positive, ended negative	+	-	—

Chapter Summary

Customer service stars have an intense desire to exceed their customers' expectations. They do this by:

◆ Becoming internally motivated to serve.

◆ Conveying a sincere interest in others.

◆ Maintaining a positive attitude.

◆ Remaining energized and enthusiastic.

◆ Knowing their organizations inside and out.

◆ Tracking their own performance.

◆ Taking initiative.

True service stars maintain these characteristics all day long by engaging in positive self-talk, taking care of their health, and developing a sense of humor.

7

Self-Check: Chapter 7 Review

Develop an action plan for becoming a customer service star.

1. Name one thing you can do this week to improve your internal motivation to serve your customers.

   _____

   _____

2. Name one thing you can do this week to convey an interest in your customers.

   _____

   _____

3. Name one thing you can do this week to keep your attitude positive.

   _____

   _____

4. Name one thing you can do this week to remain energized and enthusiastic.

   _____

   _____

5. Name one thing you can do this week to learn more about your organization.

   _____

   _____

6. Name one thing you can do this week to encourage customer feedback.

_____

_____

7. Name one thing you can do this week to take initiative when helping a customer.

_____

_____

7

Chapter *Eight*

The Team Approach to Customer Service

Chapter Objectives

▶ Communicate with others in your organization about your customers' concerns, comments, and expectations.

▶ Develop team strategies that best serve your customers.

▶ Describe how *outer-circle* elements of service give your organization a competitive edge.

The pace in today's world of customer service is unbelievably fast, and the pressure is constantly high. Whether you're dealing with internal or external customers, by phone or face-to-face, success must follow success, customer after customer. You can't make up for giving poor service to one customer by giving great service to the next customer. The damage has been done.

Many employees make a common error. They are more concerned about their job functions than their customers. The customer is the reason you have a job. Focus your attention on your customer, not your job function.

Putting the customer first means maintaining consistently high-quality standards, and to do this, you need to share your commitment to exceptional customer service with your coworkers. You need to gain their support to help deliver exceptional customer service every day, in every contact, with every customer.

Developing Team Strategies

Simply put, taking a *team approach* to customer service means working together as a group with common expectations and goals. The team approach allows growth at every level. The success of long-time service stars inspires new members of the team, and at the same time, stars gain fresh perspectives from new team members. Everyone learns, and everyone wins.

Here are some strategies to help you and your team provide exceptional customer service together:

◆ **Show pride in yourself and your coworkers.** Celebrate others' successes. Let the customer know you're proud. This ensures a much more positive experience for your customer and for you.

◆ **Be a customer advocate in your organization.** You are the voice of your organization, but you can also be the voice of the customer to your organization. Argue on your customer's behalf. Volunteer to do a service brainstorming session with your internal customers to share your perspective with other departments.

◆ **Keep the supervisors informed and learn from them.** Supervisors are a tremendous internal resource for information on the customer and your organization.

◆ **Support your teammates with information.** Share what you know freely with your coworkers. Use huddles—brief, informal meetings—instead of formal meetings when time is limited.

◆ **Discuss new policies.** Discuss any new policies with your team and create a way to explain changes to the customers in a positive way. Develop a basic script you can use initially so you don't stumble over your words. A script can also ensure that everyone is following the same plan.

◆ **Identify areas for improvement.** Your team can generate ideas on how to better serve the customer. Let ideas flow without judgment. Even the craziest ideas sometimes turn out to be the ideas that work.

> Simply put, taking a *team approach* to customer service means working together as a group with common expectations and goals.

8

Identify and then track the areas for improvement, such as realistic response times and sales. Set goals—determine what's expected of you as an individual and what's expected of the team. Coach each other, drawing on everyone's experiences and strengths.

Take a Moment

Most organizations recognize that they need your perspective. Give a presentation for the other departments about what you are learning from your customers. Do not use the presentation as an opportunity to complain. Use it as an opportunity to deliver feedback. Providing other areas of the company with appropriate feedback will enhance your value and increase your level of respect. Make the presentation positive, informative, and factual, and provide solutions that are workable.

Delivering Outer-Circle Service

With all things being equal, there is little difference between your organization and the competition. Now is the time to take your service delivery to the next level.

The *inner circle* of customer service is made up of the basic services and products your organization and your competition provides.

We can look at customer service as consisting of two circles. The *inner circle* is made up of the basic services and products your organization and your competition provides. Customers expect the services and products in the inner circle. Figure 1 illustrates the types of services customers usually expect as part of the inner circle.

Inner Circle
- Convenient hours of operation
- Toll-free phone number
- Accurate and timely billing process
- Adequate automation/ computer system
- Convenient location
- Shipping services

Figure 1

The *outer circle* allows you to differentiate your organization, to set yourself apart from the competition by providing elements that exceed your customers' expectations, as illustrated in Figure 2. Customer service stars are outer-circle fanatics.

Your *outer circle* of service allows you to set yourself apart from the competition by providing elements that exceed your customers' expectations.

Inner Circle
- Convenient hours of operation
- Toll-free phone number
- Accurate and timely billing process
- Adequate automation/ computer system
- Convenient location
- Shipping services

Outer Circle
- Customer follow-up
- Guaranteed appointment times
- Personal service from govern- ment agencies
- Child care for shoppers

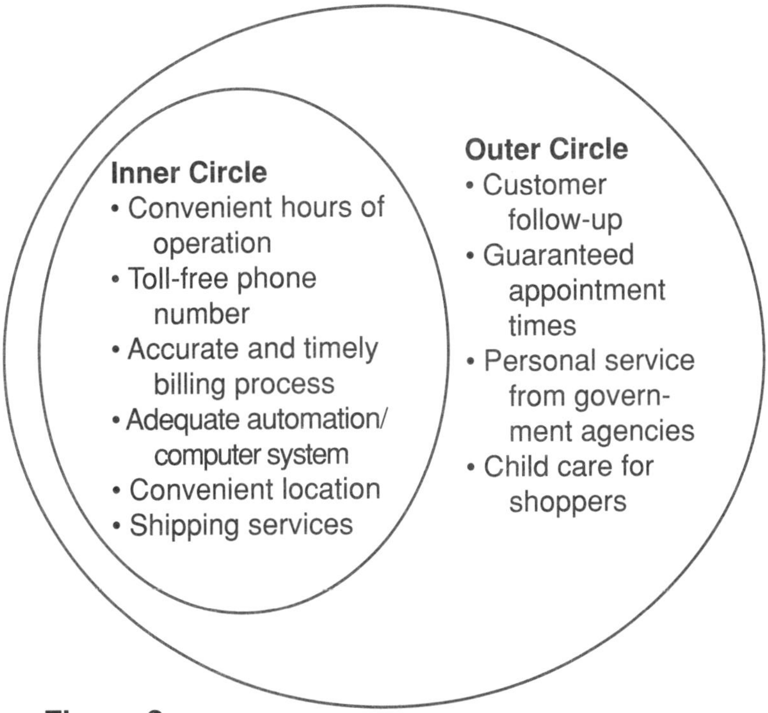

Figure 2

Here are some examples of outer-circle service:

■ A hospital sends a new mother flowers after a baby is born, but not at the same time everyone else does. They send the flowers 30 days after the birth. This is the perfect time, because all the flowers she received earlier are gone, and the exhaustion that accompanies having a new baby has set in. The new mother really appreciates this thoughtful gesture, and it comes at a time when she doesn't expect it.

■ A dentist's office located in a mall gives a waiting family member a pager. This allows the family member to shop while the patient is having dental work completed.

8

Without strong outer-circle service, you may not be offering the customer anything special enough to set you apart from the competition.

How important is outer-circle service? Extremely important. Your inner circle may be perfect. You may do everything the customer expects, but that might not be enough to guarantee that the customer will come back. Without strong outer-circle service, you may not be offering the customer anything special enough to set you apart from the competition. You may also be in a business where your customer might not understand your inner circle. In this case, your outer circle has to be outstanding.

■ When I receive health care services, I am receiving care that I am not qualified to judge. The inner circle—top-quality medical care—although extremely important, is not how I judge the service I receive. At the moment I am receiving care, I judge the outer-circle elements: how friendly the receptionist was, how long I had to wait to see the doctor, and whether the doctor has a good bedside manner and took time to answer my questions. As my health improves following the treatment, I am better able to judge if the medical care is top-quality.

Take a Moment

Meet with your team every 90 days to discuss outer-circle ideas. Why meet every 90 days? Outer-circle services become inner-circle services when customers begin to expect them from your organization, or your competition begins to offer the same services. After a while, it's not unique. By continually updating your outer circle, you will delight your customer.

What if management doesn't support your customer service initiatives? Don't give up. Work within your service team for support and encouragement. Despite your frustration, each day you will still have pride in a job well done. By your efforts, management may even realize that excellent service pays off by increasing sales and developing a loyal customer base. And who knows? One of your customers may be so impressed by your initiative that he or she may offer you a better position.

It's the little things that make the big things possible. Only close attention to the fine details of any operation makes the operation first class.

J. Willard Marriott

Cross-Selling and Up-Selling

These two techniques provide opportunities to better serve both your customer and your organization. If your organization's sales and customer service functions are separate, your knowledge of the available products and services can benefit your customers. Many companies have combined service and sales so the customer does not get bounced around.

Cross-Selling

Cross-selling is selling those accessories or services that complement the product the customer has already purchased. Let's say your customer orders a bicycle tire. You know your company offers a tool that makes installation of the tire easier. By telling your customer about the features of this tool, you are finding ways to further benefit your customer. To help you in your cross-selling efforts:

1. **Keep a log of the type of calls you receive.** Decide which ones provide sales opportunities.

2. **Determine what the customer needs.** Is it an additional service or product? Does your customer have the necessary tools, equipment, or information?

3. **Offer the materials or services to ensure that your customer's expectations are met.** Create a win-win situation by solving your customer's current or potential problem.

When you first begin cross-selling, develop a script to help you get started. That way you won't get flustered or forget important points when describing a product or service.

Cross-selling is selling those accessories or services that complement the product the customer has already purchased.

8

Up-Selling

Up-selling is
selling a
product or
service that
provides
additional
benefits at a
greater cost.

Up-selling is selling a product or service that provides additional benefits at a greater cost. If the requested product or service is not appropriate to meet the customer's needs, offer one that is. Use active listening to determine the best product fit for your customer. Be sure to give the customer all the information needed to make a good decision, including the price difference between the requested and the suggested products.

Service stars are always looking for ways to benefit the customer. Cross-selling and up-selling are additional ways to enhance your customer's service experience.

> Quality doesn't mean we have to be 100 percent better in any one thing; it means we strive to be 1 percent better in 100 things.
>
> *Jan Carlzon*

Taking Small Steps

Taking small steps will actually be faster, easier, and more effective than waiting for that one time when everything is absolutely perfect and trying to make a spectacular leap. Instead of making one customer exceptionally satisfied, try to make each customer a little more satisfied. Here are three things you can do:

◆ **Look for 1-percent improvements.** Remember, even among service stars, there is always room for improvement.

◆ **Listen to your own complaints.** Customers probably have the same complaints about your organization that you have about other organizations and maybe even your own.

◆ **Take initiative.** Reading this book and putting your new customer service skills into action is a great start. Get additional training. Accept empowerment—and act on behalf of your customer.

This is only the beginning. Think about the things you have learned and adapt them for use in your organization. Take care of your customers, both internal and external. Embrace the idea of service with heart. In the competitive environment, exceptional customer service is an absolute.

Excellence is achieved when you master the basic rules of customer service. Ask yourself, "What can I do to ensure exceptional customer service and inspire those around me to do the same?" Customer service stars aren't born; they take the initiative to learn, practice, and lead others. You can be a service star too!

Chapter Summary

Taking a *team approach* to customer service means working together as a group with common expectations and goals. Team strategies include:

- Showing pride in yourself and your coworkers.

- Being a customer advocate.

- Keeping supervisors informed and learning from them.

- Discussing new policies.

- Identifying areas for improvement.

Working as a team will allow you to move beyond *inner-circle service*—the aspects of customer service that all customers expect—to truly exceptional *outer-circle service*. Outer-circle service will delight your customers and make your organization stand out from the competition.

Two ways that you can better serve your customers and your organization are to engage in cross-selling—selling those accessories or services that complement the product the customer has already purchased—and up-selling—selling a product or service that provides additional benefits at a greater cost.

8

Self-Check: Chapter 8 Review

Answers to the following questions may be found on page 95.

1. Taking a team approach to customer service means working

   together as a group with _____

   _____ and _____.

2. What is *cross-selling?*

   _____

   _____

3. What is *up-selling?*

   _____

   _____

4. List the specific items that make up your organization's inner
   circle:

   _____

   _____

   _____

   _____

5. List the specific acts you do (or could do) that make up your
   outer circle:

   _____

   _____

   _____

   _____

Answers to Selected Exercises

Chapter 1

Take a Moment (page 16)

1. There is no right or wrong answer to this question; however, the most common answer is c, "both." We all serve people both inside and outside our organizations with information, products, and services. If you answered "internal" or "external," you may want to reexamine your definition of your customers.

2. If you can honestly answer a, "feel better," that's very good. But it may not be enough.

3. b. and c. The correct answers are 24 to 48 hours. However, never disappoint the customer. If you know it's going to take 48 hours, don't tell her or him 24.

4. b. Customers are sometimes right. In some circumstances, the customer may not be right, but *the customer is always the customer.* Whether right or wrong, treat the customer with dignity and respect.

5. e. Customer perception is the answer. Even if you are giving a great product at a great price, supported by outstanding customer service, if the customer's perceptions are negative, you're fighting a losing battle.

Chapter Review (page 18)

1. Your *internal customers* are the individuals or departments within your organization who use your products or services.

2. Your *external customers* are the persons or organizations who purchase and use your products and services.

3. When we provide *exceptional customer service,* we exceed customer expectations, demonstrate that the organization cares for the customer, and work immediately and decisively on the customer's behalf.

4. *Customer expectations* are what a customer wants before a transaction.

91

5. *Customer perceptions* are based on how your service measures up against customer expectations.

6. Exceptional Customer Service = <u>Perception</u> - <u>Expectations</u>

7. A caring and friendly atmosphere, ownership of problems, and quick solutions are all positive points of contact that work to create a good impression.

Chapter 2

Chapter Review (page 30)

1. As customers have more and more contacts with your organization, they combine their perceptions of those contacts into an overall impression of your organization's customer service. This impression is the customer's *total service experience.*

2. The customer decides.

3. a. What results does my customer want?
   b. How can I help my customer get these results?

4. Positive attitude

5. False—never yell at a customer, even if that customer is yelling at you.

Chapter 3

Chapter Review (page 44)

1. Service with heart focuses on what the customer <u>thinks</u>, <u>wants</u>, and <u>feels</u>.

2. You can't provide service with heart unless you maintain a <u>positive</u> <u>attitude</u> toward all your customers.

3. Choose from:
   a. Use the customer's name and title.
   b. Build rapport with your customers.
   c. Avoid jargon.
   d. Display confidence.

    e. Show empathy.
    f. Mirror the customer's speech and body language.

4. <u>Hearing</u> is the physical act of processing sounds.
<u>Active listening</u> means trying to find the real meaning of the words and the unspoken message behind them.

5. a. Be ready to listen.
    b. Be ready to take notes when appropriate.
    c. Show you are listening.
    d. Ask questions.
    e. Restate the customer's points.

Chapter 4

Chapter Review (page 54)

1. a. The customer didn't get what was promised or what was expected.
    b. Someone was rude to the customer.
    c. Someone was indifferent to the customer.
    d. No one listened to the customer.

2. False—Angry customers need to vent. Telling them to calm down will only make matters worse.

3. True

4. Signal, Take control, Opposite, Practice

5. Acknowledging a customer's emotions helps a customer feel <u>valued</u> and allows you to <u>develop a partnership</u> with the customer.

Chapter 5

Take a Moment (page 61)

1. Thanks the customer:
"Thank you for bringing this to our attention, Mr. Wong."

2. Empathizes with the customer:
"I can see why you might believe you would receive a service plan with your copier."

3. Reviews alternatives and offers the best solution:
   "I think our best option is to remove the fee for the labor and charge you only for the parts."

4. Educates and informs the customer:
   "Even with a service agreement, you would be charged for the parts."

5. Arranges for follow-up:
   "Would you prefer to have a sales representative stop by your office . . . or would you rather I called and discussed your options?"

Chapter Review (page 65)

1. When we try to anticipate problems and solve them before they start, we are taking a <u>proactive</u> approach to problem solving.

2. Building expectations in your customers can help you avoid the customer <u>dissatisfaction</u> that leads to complaints.

3. False—You should always involve the customer in the problem-solving process and choose the solution that will be most convenient for her or him.

4. False—If a customer asks to speak to your supervisor, ask that person to provide you with information so that you can transfer him or her to the right person. Once you have the information, if you are able to solve the problem, offer to do so.

5. True

Chapter 6

Chapter Review (page 71)

1. Exceptional customer service requires excellent telephone customer service skills. If you don't believe that your phone skills are excellent, don't panic. Use this quiz as an opportunity to identify areas in which you can improve.

2. Providing one voice for your customers means transferring them as infrequently as possible. Ask yourself what you can do to decrease your number of transfers.

3. If you are receiving a large number of transferred calls, perhaps you can provide other team members with information in advance so they won't need to transfer to you so often.

4. You and your team members should not transfer a customer more than three times. If you are the third person your customer has talked to, do not transfer the customer again. Learn whatever you can about the situation and agree on a time when you can call the customer back with an answer.

5. Your best alternative is to not put a customer on hold at all. What can you do to reduce the number of times you use your hold button?

6. Never leave a customer on hold for more than 45 seconds without returning for an update.

7. You should always ask if you can put a customer on hold and then wait for his or her response.

8. Practice saying your standard phone greeting until you can hear each word clearly. If possible, tape yourself and ask a friend to listen.

Chapter 8

Chapter Review (page 90)

1. Taking a team approach to customer service means working together as a group with <u>common expectations</u> and <u>goals</u>.

2. *Cross-selling* is selling those accessories or services that complement the product the customer has already purchased.

3. *Up-selling* is selling a product or service that provides additional benefits at a greater cost.

4. Answers will vary.

5. Answers will vary.